DEVELOPMENT OF THE BALTIC ARMED FORCES IN LIGHT OF MULTINATIONAL DEPLOYMENTS

Introduction.

The issue of transformation and of national participation in the North Atlantic Treaty Organization (NATO) and coalition alliance operations is a very important one for the three Baltic States of Estonia, Latvia, and Lithuania. Since those nations became independent of the Soviet Union in 1990-91, they have all had to build Western-style armed forces from scratch. As they were determined to become a full part of the West and to join NATO and the European Union (EU), all three nations embarked on a process of engagement with NATO and EU nation allies to create armed forces that were fully compatible with NATO and to build armed forces that would be capable of making a significant contribution to Western security. In their 2 decades of independence, the three Baltic States have adopted a policy to commit their military forces as well as civilian expertise in support of the United Nations (UN), NATO, and coalition operations in peacekeeping and active combat roles. The Baltic States have engaged in such operations for several reasons: first to demonstrate their commitment as full partners in NATO and the EU; and second, to use their participation in overseas deployments to build up experience in their own forces in order to make them fully interoperable with NATO and EU allies.[1]

This subject is also important for the U.S. military, for almost all major operations conducted over the last 3 decades, from Operation DESERT STORM in 1991, to Somalia (1991-94) to operations in the former Yugoslavia (1995-present) to the Iraq conflict and counterinsurgency (2003-11) and the ongoing operations in Afghanistan (2001-present), have been carried out as coalition operations, with dozens of NATO and non-NATO allies participating. Many of the allies in the U.S.-led and NATO-led coalition operations have been from small countries such as the Baltic States. Because small nations can and have made valuable contributions to these Western coalition operations, it is important for the U.S. military to understand the small nation perspective and experience. It is also important for the United States that small nations develop effective force transformation processes, so that they will be able to be fully interoperable with NATO and allied forces in future operations.

The Baltic States make an excellent case study to understand the role of small nations in peacekeeping, peace enforcement, and counterinsurgency operations, because they have been active participants in almost all of the operations noted previously. Somalia is the only place where the Baltic States were not present. There is ample literature on the experience of the Baltic States in coalition deployments. The Baltic Defence College, the military staff college of the three Baltic States, encourages research and publication on this subject from officers and civilian officials who have taken part in the deployments. In 2010 and 2011, the Baltic Defence College also hosted workshops on the experience of small state deployments. Furthermore, the Latvian National Defence Academy's Master of Arts (MA) program has fostered MA theses on the subject of the small state deployment experience. Finally, the three journals and official publications of the Baltic States have published some assessments of their experience in overseas deployments. This monograph is largely built upon briefings, reports, and pre-

2

sentations from company and field grade officers of the Latvian, Lithuanian, and Estonian armed forces that have experienced deployments as members of multinational operations during the last 15 years. Officers from the Baltic States have served as staff officers and unit commanders in NATO peacekeeping operations in Kosovo and Bosnia, in the Allied Coalition Forces in Iraq, and with the NATO forces deployed to the ongoing mission in Afghanistan. Most of the officers who contributed reports on their experience are students or fellow faculty members of the Baltic Defence College, which is the staff college and school for higher military education for the three Baltic States. Some of these reports were completed at my request. In other cases, the information comes from the 2010 workshop that was sponsored by the Baltic Defence College on the subject of the nation deployment experience.[2]

Nations such as Estonia, Latvia, and Lithuania might be small and have small armed forces, but even small nations can bring useful capabilities and niche forces to a military operation. In Afghanistan, Iraq, and similar operations, conflict is not characterized by the division and corps operations of a conventional state-on-state war, such as the conflict against Iraq in 1991 and 2003. Recent operations in counterinsurgency environments are characterized by battalion, company, and and even small forces spread out in small towns and rural areas carrying out operations to secure the local population, to support nation building efforts, and to train the host nation forces. In such a conflict, a well-trained team or company from a small nation can be just as effective on the ground as a team or company from the United States or a larger NATO ally.

The experience of the Baltic States is also an important part in the study of the transformation process as it applies to smaller nations. The three Baltic States made a policy of participation in active operations with NATO and Western coalition partners a central part of their program to develop, modernize, and adapt their armed forces to be fully capable Western forces. Transformation for smaller nations is vitally important because small nations such as the three Baltic States have no realistic options for national defense other than through cooperative efforts and alliance with major partners. Yet, effective cooperation and support from partners requires that the small nation understand the doctrine and tactics of the larger partners and be fully able to have its forces operate in concert with allies. One of the central goals of the Baltic States in deploying forces on active operations was to ensure interoperability with NATO and allied partners at every level and on every kind of operation. Indeed, in this respect, the three Baltic States can be rated as highly successful in the transformation process.

In terms of transformation, NATO has also been transforming since the end of the Cold War and the re-independence of the three Baltic States. While still maintaining a conventional war deterrent, and with defense of alliance territory as the first priority, NATO has also transformed into an alliance with extensive out-of-area responsibilities and connections. Stability in Africa, the Middle East, and Southeast Europe is of direct concern to Europe, so NATO has become highly involved in peacekeeping, military assistance, peace enforcement, and counterinsurgency missions outside the alliance area over the last 2 decades. The operations in Kosovo, in Afghanistan, and recently in Libya are examples of the "new" kind of operations NATO is conducting. As NATO transforms as an alliance, the armed forces of its members have had to transform as well.[3] Because of NATO's transformation, Estonia, Latvia, and Lithuania have had to develop expertise on Central Asia and other areas far outside what might be considered their natural area of concern.

More than 30 nations participated in the U.S.-led coalition in Iraq from 2003-11. Among those nations were hundreds of troops and specialist personnel from the three Baltic States. More than 30 nations have participated in the NATO force in Afghanistan since 2001. Among the forces in the NATO coalition in Afghanistan, the three Baltic States of Latvia, Estonia, and Lithuania were again present. In 2010, at the peak of the Baltic States' involvement in Afghanistan, there were more than 750 personnel, mostly military and police, present in the country as part of the NATO force. In terms of the operation, this is not an insignificant contribution. The contributions from nations such as the Baltic States can be important to the overall success of a major NATO operation.

Although the Baltic States are small, they have supplied NATO and coalition partners with highly capable fighting units, special operations detachments, medical units, munitions disposal units, and special training for almost 20 years. In Afghanistan, Lithuania took a major role as the lead nation for a provincial reconstruction team (PRT), one of 26 in the country.

In short, small nation participation has more than a political significance. As this monograph will emphasize, small nations bring genuine and useful capabilities to a conflict. Because operations such as the Kosovo peace enforcement operation and the NATO actions in Afghanistan are ongoing, and there will likely be more such coalition operations in the future. Thus, it is important for the United States, as the senior partner in NATO, to have a sound understanding of the smaller allied nations and the unique operational problems they face when deployed to serve alongside the United States and NATO forces in combat operations. In the future, the United States will need to ensure that the contribution of small nation forces is used efficiently. For their part, smaller NATO allies such as the Baltic States should evaluate their strengths and weaknesses in the light of their recent operational experience in order to develop the most effective doctrine, training, forces structure, and equipment for future coalition operations.

The focus of this monograph is on the operational deployments of the three Baltic States' armed forces and the operational lessons learned from these coalition deployments. The core assumption of this analysis is that peace enforcement and security operations such as the UN/NATO mission in Kosovo, the U.S.-led coalition force in Iraq, and the NATO coalition force in Afghanistan will be likely in the future. Therefore, it is important to continue to revise and develop the doctrine for such multinational operations. This monograph will not delve into the grand strategic debate as to whether the United States, NATO, and the West in general ought to take part in peacekeeping, or peace enforcement, or counterinsurgency operations. These operations, and a coalition approach to them, have been around for more than 6 decades, and there is no evidence that the need for stability and counterinsurgency operations will go away. If such operations continue, it is also a U.S. preference to conduct operations of this nature as part of a multinational coalition. As for the Baltic States, all three Baltic States have NATO membership at the core of their security policy. These nations are all part of the EU as well. The national governments of Latvia, Estonia, and Lithuania have made it clear in repeated statements that they will support all NATO operations and EU operations to the best of their ability.[4]

This analysis seeks to answer some key questions about the experience of the Baltic States' troop deployments on multinational operations. What are the most effective contributions made by the Baltic States to multinational forces? What have been the strengths of the Baltic armed forces in multinational operations? What have been the major limitations of the Baltic forces in multinational operations? How can multinational command and control and planning be improved to maximize the capabilities of the Baltic forces?

This monograph is organized around several major issues central to coalition operations. These are pre-deployment training, force organization, operational coordination with major coalition partners, force equipment, logistics and doctrine development.

Background: The Development of the Baltic Armed Forces.

The three Baltic States regained their independence from the Soviet Union in 1991. At the time of independence, Estonia, Latvia, and Lithuania were impoverished states that had inherited a broken Soviet economic system and little else. The armed forces of the three Baltic States had to be built from scratch. There were a few officers who had deserted from the old Soviet Army and made their way home, and there were many eager recruits who wanted to serve a new and independent nation. Otherwise, there was no equipment and little infrastructure, as the Soviet troops remained in bases in the Baltic States until 1994. What military infrastructure that was inherited was in ruins.

Although the three Baltic nations lacked money and infrastructure in the early 1990s, they had considerable advantages in terms of human capital. The three Baltic nations had highly literate and well-educated populations, and had long been the most economically developed region of the Soviet Union in terms of high tech industries. This situation dates back to the old Russian empire to which the three Baltic nations had belonged, then, the Baltic nations and Finland were the most educated and advanced regions of the empire. The troops that came to the three Baltic armed forces were excellent human material; well-educated and able to handle modern technology. The three nations adapted quickly to the Western market economy as well.

From the beginning, the three Baltic States had decided upon national strategies and policies of complete integration with the West. These included immediate development of Western democratic states, free market economies, and full membership in the EU and NATO. At first, the major NATO nations were reluctant to become openly engaged in any military support to countries that had been former Soviet republics. Instead, the three Baltic States received military training and assistance from the Nordic nations (Norway, Sweden, Denmark, and Finland) in the early 1990s. The Nordic nations provided both military equipment and training teams.[5] By 1994, the Russian Army had withdrawn from the Baltic States, and the three nations were well on their way to building regular armed forces on the Western model. Military academies were created. First battalions and then larger units stood up, and promising officers were sent to Western nations' staff colleges, including the United States, France, Germany, Denmark, Finland, and Sweden. Through the first decade of independence, the support from the Nordic nations was especially important, as those nations were generous in providing equipment, instructors, training teams, and advisors. In Estonia, the Finnish armed forces set up noncommissioned officer (NCO) instruction. Thus, for a decade, the Baltic nations received excellent professional assistance from highly-developed Western armed forces that set a solid foundation for the entry of Latvia, Estonia, and Lithuania into NATO and the EU.[6]

In 1999, the three Baltic nations formed a staff college that would handle all higher officer education for the three countries — the Baltic Defence College in Tartu, Estonia. The college was originally staffed with officers from NATO and the Nordic nations as faculty, with all instruction conducted exclusively in English. Indeed, the commitment to NATO and the West was so strong that English was decided on as the second language of the armed forces, and instruction in English was stressed for all ranks and levels of the three Baltic armed forces. The commitment to English was part of the policy of the three nations to create armed forces that were fully interoperable with the West.[7]

The three Baltic nations have small armed forces, but with a highly trained and professional cadre. In the first decade of the 21st century, Lithuania and Latvia decided on professional armed forces, while Estonia retained a conscription system. On military and security issues, the three nations cooperated closely, not only building a joint staff college and institution of higher military education, but also coordinating their officer and NCO training and holding joint exercises, with all Baltic nations participating. The defense ministers and military chiefs of the three Baltic States meet quarterly to discuss military policy issues.

Taking part in Western military operations as part of deployed peacekeeping forces was seen as a means of giving the Baltic armed forces operational experience. Actual deployments would not only provide experience for the leaders, but would also provide lessons in Western methods and doctrines for the leadership of the armed forces. The participation of Baltic forces in support of NATO, UN, and EU operations would also be a means of demonstrating the Baltic States' commitment to Western collective security.[8] In 1994, Baltic active engagement with the Western nations began with the commitment of small teams of Baltic armed forces personnel on UN peace missions. The involvement grew as the Baltic armed forces grew, and in the 1990s, Baltic teams, and later small units, served in Bosnia, Kosovo, and on UN missions.[9]

In 2004, the three Baltic nations joined both the EU and NATO as full members. That the three nations could meet both EU and NATO standards for membership after only 13 years of independence shows the full commitment they had made to become members of the Western alliance and to participate in Western collective security. With NATO membership also came commitments to support Western operations. All three Baltic nations supported the U.S.-led coalition in Iraq and contributed detachments to that mission. Latvia and Lithuania contributed company-sized units that operated with the multinational division in Iraq. Baltic officers also served as part of training teams and coalition staffs. The Baltic forces' commitment to NATO and EU missions was made with the understanding that the contribution of the three nations was to earn a "place at the table" in NATO and EU decisionmaking. The Baltic States could not expect to be taken seriously or listened to unless a serious and highly visible contribution was put forward for the collective security of NATO and the EU.[10]

The deployment of forces abroad in support of NATO and international coalition missions fits well into the Baltic national security strategies. The Lithuanian National Security Strategy of 2002 (before officially joining NATO) stated that:

> The Republic of Lithuania considers international security indivisible and seeks its own security as an indispensable part of the wider regional, European and global security of the community of nations.[11]

The *Estonian Long Term Defence Development Plan 2009-2018* published by the Estonian Defence Ministry restates the Estonian Parliament's Law of 2004, which says that:

> Estonian defence policy is based on . . . indivisibility of security, solidarity and cooperation, . . . Collective security, support to European Union capabilities in the framework of European Security and Defence Policy.[12]

The Defence Ministry furthermore asserts that Estonia's membership in NATO is one of the two pillars of national security, the other being national self-defense.[13] Since joining NATO, the three Baltic States have all taken their alliance responsibilities very seriously. The three states all strive to meet the NATO national budget goal of 2 percent of gross domestic product (GDP) for defense.[14]

Overview of Baltic Troop Deployments.

Estonia sent peacekeepers to Croatia (1995), Bosnia and Herzegovina (since 1996, officers), Lebanon (1996-97), the Middle East to support the UN Truce Supervision Organization (UNTSO) monitoring mission (since 1997), and Kosovo (since 1999, currently staff officers).

The Estonians served in Iraq from 2003-09. At the peak of operations, the Estonians had 40 personnel and served under American command. In Iraq, Estonia lost 2 soldiers killed in action, and 18 were wounded in action. The Estonians have also served in Afghanistan since 2003 and have rotated reinforced infantry companies into the country assigned to the British-led forces. In addition, Estonia has sent additional staff officers and personnel to Implementation Force (IFOR) and civilians and military and police personnel to support teams training the Afghan forces and government personnel. The Estonian commitment in Afghanistan is ongoing. Since 2010, Estonia has participated in the EU security and anti-piracy operation in the Gulf of Aden, notably in the EU mission Operation ATALANTA. Estonia has provided a ship protection team for those operations.

Lithuania first sent 90 personnel overseas to serve as peacekeepers in Croatia from 1994 to 1996. After 1996, the Lithuanians participated in the UN operations in Bosnia and Kosovo, and a team of Lithuanians also served on the Georgia observer mission. In Iraq from 2003 to 2007, the Lithuanian Army maintained a force of 120 soldiers serving under the Danish and Polish headquarters. Since 2002, the Lithuanians have had troops in Afghanistan. They have provided a highly capable special operations team as well as more than 180 personnel to run a PRT.[15]

The Latvian Army has also been active in deployments. From 2003 to 2008, Latvia committed a company-sized force of 136 soldiers to serve under U.S. command. Three Latvians were killed in action and others wounded. In Afghanistan, the Latvians have maintained one company element in the country under NATO's IFOR command.

The Iraq and Afghanistan operations have been the first true combat operations for the armed forces of the three Baltic States since they regained independence. The Baltic States saw operations evolve over a period of more than a decade. The operations evolved from small teams deployed on peacekeeping and observer missions, to platoon-sized formations operating under a larger allied partner, to deployments in Iraq and Afghanistan at the size of a reinforced company formation with additional support units. As well as company-sized units, the armed forces of the three Baltic States have also deployed a variety of specialist teams in support of coalition operations. These teams include improvised explosive device (IED) detachments, medical detachments, special forces detachments, and naval security teams. Baltic nations have also contributed transport aircraft and communications teams to active coalition operations. Civilian trainers, especially police trainers, as well as aid workers have also been part of the Baltic States' commitment to coalition and NATO operations, especially in the case of Afghanistan, where all three Baltic States have also deployed a small number of civilian experts to support the coalition nation-building program.[16] In 2010, the three Baltic States had more than 750 personnel, including civilian government specialist personnel and military personnel, serving in Afghanistan. Taken as a whole, this represents a significant commitment of personnel and resources for three small countries. To get some idea of the effect of the deployments on a small nation's armed forces, one can take the example of Estonia, a country of 1.35 million people with a peacetime armed forces of 5,500 personnel and a wartime armed forces of 16,000 (planned to expand to 25,000 by 2018). In 2009 they deployed two infantry companies and support elements to Afghanistan—a total of 300 men—which constituted 5.5 percent of the total peacetime force.[17]

Due to the long period that the Baltic nations' forces have served in Iraq and Afghanistan, the majority of the officers and NCOs of the armed forces of the three nations have now served at least one rotation period of 6 months in a combat zone. Many of the career cadre have seen multiple tours in both Iraq and Afghanistan. In short, the Baltic armed forces have gained considerable warfighting experience in the last decade. Baltic national personnel have had the opportunity to serve with key partner nations on deployments that include serving with the United States, United Kingdom (UK), Denmark, Italy, and Norway.

Lessons Learned from Baltic Deployments
Pre-deployment Training.

One of the key—but unspoken—aspects of the policy of the three Baltic States to deploy forces on overseas missions was to prove to NATO and the EU that the three Baltic nations, as aspiring members of the EU and NATO before 2004, were capable of making a genuine contribution to the military operations of the Western Alliance. This also meant a national commitment to see that any personnel deployed were carefully selected and fully prepared to carry out their mission. To ensure the success of this commitment, each national armed force had to prepare and execute a pre-deployment training program.

Sending even small numbers of troops to support an observer or peacekeeping mission pushed the Baltic States to ensure that all the personnel deployed were fully prepared to carry out the mission. In each country the armed forces coordinated with NATO nations that were highly experienced in such missions. In this regard, Denmark was especially helpful in sending special training teams to prepare deploying personnel. The Baltic nations also drew on the national universities for support in training the deploying personnel in the language and culture of the nation where they would serve. In addition, upon its founding in 1999, the Baltic Defence College, as the institution of higher military education of the three Baltic States, placed a strong emphasis on peacekeeping and low intensity conflict into the curriculum for its captains' course, its joint staff course, and its colonels' course. Exercises emphasizing peacekeeping and peace enforcement operations became a major part of the Baltic Defence College courses, with the expectation that the Baltic officers would be likely to deploy on such operations.

In general, in the period from 1991 to 2002, the Baltic States emphasized unit training of their national armies, which were generally composed of light infantry and mechanized infantry forces. The goal of the national training programs was to develop companies, battalions, and brigades that would be interoperable with NATO forces in small and large operations.

English language training has been an important part of the Baltic military education process. The three

Baltic military academies all teach English and stress a high level of competence. Prior to deployment, all Baltic personnel are given additional English instruction to ensure that they will be able to communicate easily in the NATO command language. Effective operations in a multinational environment require good English skills.[18] Since 1999, all staff courses taught at the Baltic Defence College require officers and civilian officials to meet a NATO Standardization Agreement (STANAG) level 3 English proficiency in order to simply enroll in the courses. English language training extends down to NCO and soldier level as well, to ensure that Baltic soldiers and civilian personnel will be able to deploy and be interoperable with no language barriers in dealing with NATO or Western allies.[19] The fluency in the English language that one finds in the Baltic States, among the civilian society as well as in the military, is a symbol of the genuine transformation of the society, economy, and culture in the 2 decades since these nations regained independence. Where Russian was the second language only 20 years ago, today English is the lingua franca in all international dealings. For example, the quarterly joint meetings of the Baltic military chiefs and defense ministers are conducted in English — the only common language of the three nations (the national languages of the Baltic States are very different).

In general, the training programs of the Baltic States proved highly successful in developing effective battalions and brigades. However, the Baltic States have been limited by of the lack of experience in higher operations in general. Luckily, the Western nations, which included the United States, Germany, Denmark, Finland, Norway, Sweden, and the Netherlands, provided experienced instructors to the Baltic Defence College to train and educate the Baltic officers in operations. The operational level training was sound and adequate by any Western standard. The essential goal to provide well-trained and fully prepared infantry units to international operations was met. However, there were several problem areas noted in the training of specialist personnel and teams for active operations.

A report from an Estonian officer concerning the Estonian commitment to Afghanistan (to support the British in Helmand Province) noted that:

> Estonian and Baltic light infantry units have been able to contribute sets of skills that have superseded those of specifically designated units of allies. However, an overall understanding of and adopting a proactive approach to certain aspects and effects of high-intensity operations has been a problem area.[20]

Essentially, this meant that the deployed troops could have had a deeper understanding of counterinsurgency procedures before deploying to the area.

The problem in this case was not the training of the Estonian team of six intelligence personnel who deployed from November 2006 to March 2007. The Estonian Intelligence team had been carefully prepared by U.S. trainers, and an additional special course was conducted for the team managed by the whole Estonian Army Intelligence Battalion. Combat training of the small team was conducted by the Estonian Peace Operations Center.[21] Yet, although the unit was to be committed to support of the UK forces in Helmand, there was little coordination with the British Army before the team's deployment. The only training with UK forces was a live fire exercise and some battle drills in the UK. No human intelligence (HUMINT) specific training was offered or authorized by the UK respective branch. According to the Estonians, this led to their lack of knowledge in existing procedures, documentation, and rules within the International Security Assistance Force (ISAF), because these had not been shared with them prior to deployment. The Estonian team leader noted:

> According to MOU [Memorandum of Understanding] the unit was given OPCON under TF Helmand (UK) without any national caveats. In the good faith it was assumed that Estonian HUMINT [Estonian Human Intelligence] teams will be integrated into the TF respective system, but that never happened. Already the first unit (ESTHUMINT-1) was kept away from UK HUMINT and Counter Intelligence (CI) systems and tasks given to them were more than often just 'something to do' type.[22]

The MOU put together and agreed to by the UK and Estonia would not impose any restrictions or special conditions on the use of the team. It has been the Estonian policy, and indeed the policy of all three Baltic States, that their forces deployed to Iraq and Afghanistan are combat ready forces and can be employed in any manner deemed suitable by the task forces they are assigned to—including combat operations. All of the Baltic States had military personnel killed in Iraq and Afghanistan, and the "no caveats" policy of deployment is the norm. In this case, at the operational level it was assumed that the Estonian HUMINT team would be fully integrated with the UK forces. However, there was apparently a strong suspicion on the part of the UK commanders at the tactical level that the Estonian team was not to be used and any real cooperation was denied. Essentially, the UK forces were not familiar with the Estonian unit and its capabilities, so the unit was used very little. In fact, the HUMINT team could and should have been extensively used to support the combat units in Helmand Province. After the poorly executed deployment of the HUMINT team the Estonian team leader noted that:

> in the future all efforts should be done in highest level to enforce complete integrated training with units with whom the deployment will be conducted. Common awareness and understanding of existing rules, documents and procedures is mandatory to be introduced in pre-deployment training.[23]

Upon assuming the responsibility for leading a PRT in Afghanistan in 2005, Lithuania had to develop a cultural training program for its deploying personnel. The cultural material provided by the United States was too general and did not specifically address the issues of the Ghor Province, in west central Afghanistan, which had its own set of conditions. The Lithuanian army staff contracted the only two Dari speakers in Lithuania to provide basic language instruction to personnel before deployment to Afghanistan. In addition, the military staff worked with the national university academics to develop a cultural awareness training program specific to the province where the Lithuanians would deploy. The Lithuanian soldiers who deployed on the mission felt that they had at least a good basis to work with, but still believed that the cultural preparation could have been more extensive.[24]

Force Organization.

When the Baltic nations committed themselves to sending company-sized, and even larger, detachments to support the coalition operations in Iraq and Afghanistan, they underwent a commitment to adapt their force structure for these missions. The officers who deployed report that the key operational requirement for the Baltic contingents was that they were to be highly flexible and ready to take on more missions than assigned by the coalition commanders. That the Baltic nations could expect to take on more missions was a result of the "no caveat" policy of the three Baltic States that allow their forces to be used as the senior force commanders see fit. In fact, being ready to take on more than specifically assigned missions meant that Baltic States' units deploying to Iraq and Afghanistan had to increase the specialists and support forces to their military detachments to create balanced units capable of fulfilling a variety of missions. The additional flexibility required all three countries to spend money on communications equipment and capabilities for their forces. The Estonians added a special signals team after it first deployed forces to Afghanistan. As experience was built up, the Estonians added further units to support their infantry company operating in Helmand Province under UK command. In 2008, Estonia added a sniper team to its forces, as well as a mortar platoon. In 2009, a fire support team was added. In 2010, an anti-IED detachment was deployed.

The Lithuanians, with the experience of leading a PRT from 2005 to the present, have had to make several changes to the PRT support structure to accomplish their mission. In setting up the headquarters in the first rotation, the Lithuanians had some friction when some of the branch chiefs of the PRT staff were officers from other countries operating on a different rotation schedule than the Lithuanians. Because this required changing a branch chief in mid-rotation and other staff changes, the Lithuanians concluded that all staff branch chiefs should be from the lead country to prevent rotation conflicts such as this. The problems of the rotation schedule also applied to small national contingents working under the Lithuanians in which some national rotations occurred in the middle of the lead nation PRT rotation. The failure to coordinate rotations at first meant that the lead nation and new rotation needed "additional in theatre training, familiarization with unit procedures and so on."[25] The Lithuanian PRT chief of staff noted that units needed to follow standard operating procedures (SOPs) when deploying on an operation and should avoid development of additional SOPs.[26]

Operational Coordination with Coalition Partners.

The whole process of deploying forces on overseas missions was made easier in the 1990s by the Estonian, Latvian, and Lithuanian parliaments passing laws that authorized the deployment of national forces overseas on NATO and allied missions, and set the guidelines and conditions for the deployment of forces.[27] Thus, all the deployments of the three Baltic States since the early 1990s have taken place in conditions of full transparency and with full legitimacy, backed by parliamentary law as well as the national agreements with NATO and allied states. Under the national laws, the Baltic national forces can be deployed in combat operations without any caveats. Operating under full legality is important in democratic states, so the Baltic military staffs have ensured that the deployments are transparent to the political leadership and that the public is well informed.

Although the Baltic States do not place caveats on the use of their troops by higher allied headquarters, other nations do have caveats. One of the principles of planning Baltic deployments is a complete legal understanding of the caveats and conditions enacted by allied forces and understanding how such caveats might affect the operations. Commanders and staffs from the three Baltic States all point out the importance of pre-deployment training and close coordination with the forces of their larger partner states with which they will deploy. Pre-deployment training means holding exercises together and spending time with the larger partner's units. The Estonian HUMINT team would have been used more effectively if it had trained together with the British forces that it was assigned to support.

The Baltic States had to deal with a large number of legal issues in deploying its troops abroad. These issues included contracting services with national companies for support, as well as drawing up contracts and MOUs with host nation companies and governments. In Afghanistan, as leader of a PRT, the Lithuanian government had to negotiate an MOU with the government of Afghanistan that laid out national responsibilities in context of the Afghan national strategy.[28] Setting out an agreement covering 5 years of operations in a counterinsurgency environment was a complex task, and that Lithuania could handle such negotiations and agreements demonstrates that not only have the armed forced been transformed in their capabilities by the experience of overseas deployments, but the Lithuanian Foreign Ministry has also gained considerable experience.[29] In addition, because the Baltic States depend upon large nation support for basic logistics, including supply of food, fuel, ammunition, water, and laundry, the provision and payment for all these items and services had to be set out legally. In fact, the Baltic national staffs became competent in managing the legal and contract side of operations, with a mention from one Baltic defense ministry lawyer that, "it is sometimes not very easy for small nations such as ours to negotiate with large nations such as the US."[30]

In Iraq and Afghanistan, the Baltic forces studied and became familiar with the U.S. and UK published counterinsurgency doctrines before deployment. NATO counterinsurgency doctrine was also studied.[31] Studying doctrine and ensuring that the commanders and staff are working from the same concepts are key to effective operations in a coalition environment. Luckily, this has not been a major issue because the Baltic Defence College, which trains most of the Baltic officers above the rank of lieutenant, teaches NATO planning procedures and doctrine as well as U.S. and UK doctrine in its courses on counterinsurgency and stability operations. Baltic national contingents also stressed doctrine education in the unit preparation for Iraq and Afghanistan operations.

The Lithuanian experience is the most relevant as the Lithuanians have the most experience in multinational coordination due to their role as lead nation of a PRT. The Lithuanian experience provides some examples of the frictions that occur from various national caveats. None of the national caveats that the Lithuanians faced from their allied nations in their PRT was a show-stopper, but all of them required extra planning to make the PRT run smoothly. For example, the Danish mobile liaison observation team (MLOT) was not allowed to conduct guard duty. The Croatian MLOT was not allowed to conduct riot control tasks.

Per IFOR directions, the Lithuanian contingent was not allowed to operate outside its areas of responsibility, nor to participate in counternarcotics operations. In order to mitigate the frictions of the national caveats and of the IFOR and Afghan imposed restrictions, the caveats were made known to the Lithuanian force planners well before deployment of national contingents. Taking this information into account, the necessary tasks were allotted to the contingents within the PRT with these caveats and restrictions in mind. With good prior planning, the Lithuanians were able to maximize the force efficiency in the Ghor Province operations.[32]

Essentially, the Baltic States all worked from the understanding that they can only deploy and operate while serving under a senior partner nation and that it is their responsibility to adapt and prepare themselves to work with the senior partner—be that partner the United States, the UK, or Denmark. There was considerable friction in the first major deployments to Iraq and Afghanistan simply because deployments on a larger scale (hundreds of personnel with equipment per rotation) were situations with which the Baltic military staff simply had no experience. The Baltic States had to learn to do the complex rotation planning, force preparation, sustainment, legal support, and allied coordination with little prior background. It should be noted that most of the friction and problems noted herein occurred in the earlier force rotation; since then, the three Baltic States have gained experience.

Material and Logistics.

Issues of equipment interoperability and maintenance of support and supply can be some of the most pressing issues for small nations that participate in a NATO or multinational coalition operation. Small nations have small infrastructure, and the limited amount of support infrastructure that is available is usually not easily transported and deployed. In addition, the military staffs of small nations have very limited experience in sending forces overseas.

The Baltic nations, as is the case for all small nations, do not have the force structure or resources to send fully equipped and self-contained units to deploy thousands of miles from home and then be sustained from home. With limited transport and support services, small nations such as the Baltic States found that they needed to partner with a larger nation to deploy and sustain forces far from home.

The Baltic States have found that interoperability can be a problem—communications equipment, ammunition supply, and vehicle maintenance can be difficult, as not all the Baltic equipment is common to the larger partner nations serving in Afghanistan or Iraq. For example, a good deal of the Baltic national forces equipment comes from the Nordic nations. Vehicles tend to come from Germany. Communications equipment comes from various nations. The Baltic reports note that there have been some difficulties in achieving technical interoperability of electronic warfare (EW) systems between the Baltic States, and the United States and the UK. In addition, establishing secure radio communications with allies has been a complicated issue.[33]

Basic supply items can be a cause of friction for a small nation. Due to the variety of equipment used in the Baltic forces, keeping ammunition supplied can be an issue. In Afghanistan, some types of ammunition used by Estonian units were in limited supply, and it was difficult for the national staff to get the required ammunition to Afghanistan and then down to the unit level.[34]

Arranging for equipment maintenance and supply of spare parts can be a major headache for small nations with very limited logistics. In 2006, early in the Lithuanian deployment to Ghor Province in Afghanistan, a shortage of spare parts and vehicle maintenance problems forced the Lithuanian forces to cut back on operations until the problems were sorted out.[35]

A further important support issue for small nations is airlift. Small nations such as the Baltic States have small air forces, and of the three states only Lithuania has some transport aircraft as part of its armed forces. Thus, Estonia and Latvia depend completely upon airlift from strategic partners. In getting small shipments of parts, or small numbers of personnel to the field, Estonia and Latvia were at the mercy of the scheduling and airlift priorities of the larger nations. For the most part, the Baltic countries believe that U.S. support was good. However, the Lithuanians were very glad that they had some transport aircraft that could respond immediately to calls from the PRT in Afghanistan to bring spare parts, special teams, and rotate personnel home on leave.

Iraq and Afghanistan pressed the Baltic States to make major changes in their procurement and development policies. When the Baltic nations committed themselves to supporting the Iraq and Afghanistan coalition operations, they had to acquire appropriate uniforms and equipment for desert climates. The vehicles and heavy equipment of the Baltic States were suitable for northern European conventional operations, but not for an insurgency operation in which the main threats to personnel and vehicles were IEDs, mines, and small arms fire. With the largest commitment to Afghanistan, Lithuania went ahead and developed its own desert uniforms and personal soldier equipment. Both Lithuania and Estonia took their support vehicles, usually German-made trucks and all-terrain vehicles, and had local industries modify them for the conditions their forces were likely to face, for example, the installation of reinforced axles, spall protection lining, and safety seats.[36]

Photo provided by the Estonian Armed Forces.

Figure 1. Modified Estonian truck in Afghanistan.

Lessons Learned Process.

Learning from ongoing operations is a key part of the military process. In the first decade of standing up the brand new forces of the Baltic States, there was so much to do, yet so few trained commanders and staff officers to do it, that creating a coherent lessons learned process came in low on the list of priorities. The active experience of deploying troops to high risk operations overseas, especially to combat zones such as Iraq and Afghanistan, pushed the Baltic nations to develop a lessons learned system just for survival. With the first Baltic units deployed to peacekeeping operations in Yugoslavia in the 1990s, a regular program of reports to the national headquarters from the field was established. This relatively informal after action report (AAR) system was used to modify doctrine, equipment, and training for follow-on rotations.[37]

In their initial deployments, Estonia and Latvia relied on a fairly ad hoc process with a focus on collecting data on material and transport issues, but not on tactical lessons. Estonia deployed to high-intensity conflicts in Iraq and Afghanistan without a proper lessons learned system. Once units or detachment deployed, there was constant contact with the home forces, and there was also ongoing contact with the next rotation so as to ensure a smooth turnover.[38] Like Estonia, the Latvian approach to lessons learned has largely been ad hoc, with only a limited analysis of gained lessons and few conclusions drawn with regard to doctrine before 2010.[39] Although Estonia and Latvia have seen less systematic dissemination of lessons learned, the smallness of their forces has allowed for an informal transmission of vital information and lessons as the outgoing rotation meets with the incoming force and passes information.

In contrast to Estonia and Latvia, Lithuania, with the largest armed forces of the three Baltic States, has a well-developed formal lessons learned process. Lithuania developed a special office in the national military headquarters to collect, analyze, and quickly disseminate lessons learned on active operations. Lithuania has a developed doctrine for the AAR process, as well as a fairly developed doctrine on counterinsurgency operations.[40] Officers from all three Baltic nations agree that the deployments to the Balkans and to Iraq and Afghanistan have pushed the Baltic nations to develop their process of collecting data and learning and disseminating lessons. Doctrine is now taken very seriously in the three Baltic States, and all three nations have published manuals and handbooks on counterinsurgency doctrine, with the Lithuanian literature on the subject being the most extensive.

Lithuania and Estonia made a point of using the first officers deployed on operations as instructors in their national officer and soldier and NCO courses. The intent was to ensure that the latest operational lessons and experience were passed to the new soldiers as quickly as possible.[41] Indeed, from the first deployments, the three Baltic States have all worked to see that the recent experience and specific lessons are disseminated to the national forces as quickly as possible.

Lithuania, with the experience and responsibility of having led a PRT in Afghanistan since 2005, has gone the farthest in terms of developing doctrine. Afghanistan's experience included constant liaison with the government of Afghanistan and negotiating an MOU with the Afghan government. The PRT task was especially complex since it required multinational coordination. This meant developing an organizational structure and operating concept that included civilian personnel from Lithuania and several other nations, as well as military personnel from several nations. This experience has led Lithuanian officers to develop a doctrine on how to operate a PRT and how to conduct counterinsurgency. The Lithuanians took established

U.S. and UK counterinsurgency doctrine and added their own variations to best manage the PRT operation. The Lithuanians also developed their own approach to meet the unique requirements of the Ghor Province where they were stationed.[42]

Summary and Conclusion.

The three Baltic States, in their extensive deployments in support of NATO and allied coalitions operations, have proven that the armed forces of small states can develop and adjust rapidly and effectively. By NATO and U.S. standards, the three Baltic States have fielded personnel and units able to carry out complex tasks effectively in combat conditions. Since the 1990s, the performance of the three Baltic nations in support of UN, NATO, and allied deployments has been consistently effective. This is a remarkable accomplishment, considering that the three Baltic States started in 1991 literally from scratch — there was nothing that the Baltic nations wanted to retain from the Soviet military or its traditions. Despite the initial poverty of the three states, their lack of infrastructure, and few military traditions, the armed forces of the Baltic States developed rapidly to the point that they can now carry out highly complex tasks — such as commanding a PRT in Afghanistan. In general, the armed forces of Estonia, Latvia, and Lithuania set out with the goal of using the deployment experience to develop their forces to be interoperable with NATO. This is a goal they have met.

To answer the original questions posed in this monograph: The three Baltic States have demonstrated that small nations can commit a variety of forces and personnel to overseas operations. The three Baltic States have all deployed light infantry forces to Kosovo, Iraq, and Afghanistan. In addition, all three countries have sent training teams to train host nation personnel in several operations. Lithuania and Estonia have deployed special forces detachments to combat operations. Estonia has committed an ordnance disposal detachment to Afghanistan. Latvia and Lithuania have committed engineer and support detachments. Lithuania has committed the staff to man a PRT in Afghanistan. Just as important as the troops, the Baltic States have demonstrated the commitment and the ability to sustain those forces for many rotations. Indeed, the variety of missions that these three small states can carry out is fairly impressive. All the Baltic forces that have been deployed have been effective partners in operations. There is no single niche capability that the Baltic States have fulfilled, nor do the three states want to be in the position of being solely a niche force provider.

On the other hand, the limitations of the three Baltic States are fairly clear. The naval and air forces of the Baltic States are very limited. Only Lithuania has some air transport aircraft. All of the Baltic nations have to rely on partner states for airlift, and that is an issue that causes some problems. The logistics capability of the three Baltic States, at least their ability to sustain units outside their home countries, is minimal. This is also a problem area. Essentially, the Baltic States cannot deploy forces outside their home countries without linking themselves with a larger partner nation that can provide the airlift, logistics, and support that is required. In all cases, partner nations have come forward and handled these activities. It is important to note this, because when a small nation partners with a larger ally, extensive coordination, planning, and joint training is required to make things run smoothly. A good deal of lead time is also required to make an operation work. In the past, the Baltic States have developed good working relationships and joint training programs with larger partners such as the United States, the UK, and Denmark. For the most part, the partnerships and support have gone smoothly. However, it is essential to note that support cannot work on an ad hoc basis. If the Baltic States commit forces to a NATO reaction force for rapid deployment, there will need to be extensive pre-arrangements for logistics support from larger partners.

The deployments of the Baltic forces in the last 20 years show that small nations need to have their own capability for specialized training, cultural training, and basic HUMINT. In a diverse country like Afghanistan, each province operates under different conditions, and the ethnic and cultural differences between regions can be enormous. In short, there is no such thing as a "one size fits all" doctrine or unit preparation. The Baltic countries all found the need to develop their own specialized cultural training programs to meet the specific conditions and language issues that their forces would meet in places such as Kosovo, Iraq, and Afghanistan. All the Baltic countries used their own resources to contract for cultural, language, and specialist training. In every case, the deploying soldiers found the preparation provided by the national forces, often working with the national universities, was extremely valuable. The key lesson is that small nations have to be proactive and seize the initiative in liaising with other forces and developing the right kind of cultural and language training for their forces.

One of the major lessons in the deployment of the Baltic Forces was the importance of a mutually understood doctrine. When small nations take on significant leadership roles, as the Lithuanians have done in Afghanistan, there is a need for detailed guidance and doctrine coming from the lead country and developed in partnership with the coalition headquarters. Doctrine is even more important in NATO and EU out-of-area operations conducted today because these are not only military operations, but also have a large civilian component. All this meant that even a small nation such as Lithuania devoted a good deal of effort to creating its own doctrine and local strategy that suited its mission in the Ghor Province of Afghanistan. This was not a rejection of U.S. or UK doctrine, or an approach that went against the allied command policy in Afghanistan. It was simply meeting the need to adapt a general doctrine to the specific local requirements. Luckily, Lithuania and the other Baltic States have national staffs and well-educated field grade officers who could identify requirements quickly as issues arose during deployments and devise appropriate programs and training to meet the needs.

Because they lack mass and have very limited support capabilities, small nations must be able to adapt quickly to conditions so they can operate effectively with their allies. One senior UK officer said this of the Baltic forces:

> Do I understand this word [interoperability] properly? It seems to me that no dedicated activities are carried out to achieve it. Estonians are simply brave guys who adapt to any situation. Good enough to adapt to interoperability as well. . . .[43]

From the initial peacekeeping experience in the former Yugoslavia in the 1990s, the Baltic forces have offered a good example for other nations to follow in force development and transformation. Indeed, money and resources have not played a major role in the transformation of the forces. The Baltic States have limited resources, yet they have used what they have efficiently to the point of designing and modifying equipment needed for operations in Iraq and Afghanistan. The success of the transformation process was founded on a powerful commitment of the three Baltic States' governments to see their forces developed to NATO standards and to build armed forces, albeit small, that could still make a substantial contribution to the Western Alliance. All three armed forces stressed thorough training at every level. In addition, at every step of the Baltic deployments, starting with the 1990s, the three national military establishments carefully reviewed the lessons of each operation as they were ongoing and made rapid changes in their doctrine and forces structure and procurement with each operation. The three Baltic States have been very successful in adopting the Western military culture and ethos. Again, this was a matter of concerted national will and good leadership to make a transformation.

The Baltic experience shows that small states are able to contribute highly trained units of company or larger size able to operate under multinational command. The development of this capability is based on several factors. The success of the Baltic States' deployments as allied forces were possible because, from the start, the three states understood that they would have to serve under a lead nation that could provide the transport, command and control, and logistical support necessary. Knowing this, it was the duty of the three Baltic States to learn about and adapt to the lead nation for the operation. Getting this right required extensive planning and coordination before the deployment of the Baltic forces. It also required some training with the lead nation before deploying. Although this planning and coordination failed on a few occasions — as in the case of the Estonian HUMINT team sent to support the UK forces — for the most part, it was carried out successfully. The pre-deployment training and planning has been generally successful, and the Baltic military staffs have shown that they can carry out complex planning.

The high standard of officer and NCO education and training in the Baltic States was also key to the successful performance of the mission. The three Baltic States have formed highly effective military education institutions from the level of lieutenant to colonel. Given their limited resources, the three Baltic States maximized their personnel and infrastructure to create the Baltic Defence College, a single staff college and institute of higher military education that is equally owned by the three nations. The quality of the staff college is shown by its accreditation by the U.S. military, the Canadian armed forces, and by several other major NATO nations as being fully equivalent to their national staff courses. The colonels' course taught by the Baltic Defence College is accredited by NATO. The Baltic commanders and national staffs, manned with officers trained in the Baltic States and in NATO nations, have proven equal to the task of deploying a significant number of personnel overseas. This required numerous adaptations, including developing desert equipment for the soldiers and modifying tactical vehicles for Middle East and Central Asian conditions and counterinsurgency.

Although the Baltic States have been successful in deploying significant forces overseas, there were many areas of friction that occurred simply due to the complexity of the tasks required and the initial lack of experience of the Baltic States' forces. Developing detailed legal agreements with other nations, creating a long-term strategy for rotation of forces, arranging for logistics and support in undeveloped nations thousands of miles from home, developing training programs, developing cultural awareness programs, and developing close coordination with military partners have all been points of friction for the three small Baltic States. These are complex tasks for large nations as well. Problems in all these areas were overcome because the national staffs had well-trained staff officers, and the three Baltic States were effective in collecting lessons learned from operations as they were ongoing and quickly adapting and making changes to doctrine, procedure, and equipment to meet the mission challenges. If the well-trained staffs and an effective program to learn and disseminate lessons were not in place, the many problems that arose would not have been readily overcome.

The long-term partnering programs of the Baltic States' armed forces with older NATO nations has also been key to the successful deployments of Baltic national forces. Over 20 years, the Baltic States have built up close relationships with allies (the close relationship of the Baltic States with the Danish forces is a case in point), and these close relationships speeded the process of transformation and built up trust between the key alliance partners. Forging partnership on the battlefield can be done, but requires time and leads to less effective use of small nation forces.

How effective were the three Baltic States in using the numerous deployments on active operations as part of a program to transform their forces? By most standards, the effort must be judged as highly successful. For one thing, the overwhelming majority of officers and NCOs of the armed forces of three countries have now taken part in active operations as part of a multinational coalition force—usually operating with NATO partners. The small size of the Baltic forces meant that they had to work closely with allies on a daily basis. This means that for periods of 6-month deployments, hundreds of Baltic personnel on every rotation worked closely with partners, using the English language and operating within an allied command system. In little more than a decade, the armed forces of the three Baltic States have become highly combat experienced. Working closely in an allied environment is now an integral part of the culture and standard operations of the three Baltic nations.

Senior American and British officers who have worked with the armed forces of the Baltic States on deployments in Iraq and Afghanistan have praised the performance of the Baltic forces. One has to note that, in both cases, the Baltic States deployed forces to hot areas and fought under U.S. and British commands in tough environments—and with no caveats. All of the senior American and British officers with whom the author has spoken have a high regard for the fighting competence and professionalism of the Baltic troops. Indeed, throughout NATO, although the Baltic States forces might be small, they are highly regarded. This is solely the result of the professionalism they have demonstrated on deployment operations.

The experience of the Baltic nations in overseas deployments illustrates common problems and frictions that occur in any large multinational operation. The ways and means by which the Baltic States have overcome the problems should serve as a model for other small states in participating in future peace enforcement or stability operations in the context of a multinational environment.

Recommendations for the U.S. Land Forces.

First of all, the good news is that now and in the foreseeable future, the United States can count on military support and participation of the three Baltic States in a NATO-approved and supported military contingency operation. The three Baltic States have shown the capability to deploy well-trained and well-equipped units of company and reinforced company size (about 200 personnel) and maintain units of this size in a combat zone for 6-month rotations. However, to do this, the three Baltic States need airlift support to and from the deployment area and, when in theater, need a full array of logistics support. Both NATO and the United States will need to take this into account when planning contingency operations in the NATO area.

The best way to use the well-trained Baltic forces and to employ the several capabilities that they can bring to military operations, including infantry, explosive ordnance disposal (EOD), engineer, police training teams, medical, and HUMINT teams, would be as a single force that would work and train together. The Baltic States might consider a revival of an idea from the early 1990s when the three states created the BALTBAT, a battalion composed of troops from the three countries that trained together and was intended to support NATO or UN peace operations. In fact, the battalion was never deployed, but it did advance the training and English knowledge of the three armed forces, and it helped the three Baltic countries attain NATO levels of support in an efficient manner. The BALTBAT was an important and very successful project initiated by the three Baltic States for the transformation of their forces to NATO standards in the 1990s. Now the three Baltic States each have mature Western armed forces, so such a program today would be developed much more easily.

Since the early 1990s, the three Baltic countries have shown that they can work together with U.S. and NATO allies in multinational operations. The revival of the BALTBAT concept and the creation of a battalion-sized force for the three Baltic States with companies from each country, as well as special support detachments, including intelligence, military police, EOD, and engineer and logistics elements such as supply and medical, would not be especially difficult for the three countries as they already work together on many common military issues such as the Baltic Defence College and other joint training. This battalion would train and operate using the English language, since the Baltic States have already proven they can operate easily in English and be available on rapid notice to support a NATO contingency mission. The United States ought to encourage and support such a concept in future defense discussions within NATO.

Creation of such a force is very doable, and the costs would not be high. For the United States, it might entail some small costs in supporting training of a combined BALTBAT with partnered U.S. forces. The United States can arrange that a new BALTBAT is linked in training and planning to a U.S. brigade stationed in Europe or to a UK brigade, because for language reasons, the Baltics need to pair with an English-speaking country. Such a battalion kept at a high state of training and readiness, and including special support teams, would be a significant asset for NATO as NATO faces the post-Afghanistan contingencies that are likely to arise.

Finally, the U.S. military should consider the military and specialist civilian personnel in planning and standing up military advisory teams that would assist nations in NATO's area of interest, including Africa, the Mideast, the Caucasus, and Central Asia. As noted, the Baltic nations have armed forces with much experience in counterinsurgency operations gained in Iraq, Afghanistan, and Kosovo. Baltic nation personnel are competent, educated to a Western standard, and are fluent in English. They have a well-deserved reputation among the U.S. and British officers who have worked with them as being highly professional and easy to work with. In short, they would be a useful addition to a small advisory team trying to assist the armed forces of a small nation. Moreover, the Baltic officers, NCOs, and civilian specialists can bring the perspective of small nations that have recently gone through a process of building Western and democratic armed forces completely from scratch, and the Baltic personnel would have valuable insights in this regard. Additionally, if an advisory mission were proposed in support of the broader NATO strategy of engagement, the Baltic States would be very likely to participate. The history of Baltic States' support for NATO indicates that Baltic governments will be very willing to cooperate in such missions.

ENDNOTES

1. For a national view from the Baltic, see Toomas Riim, "Estonia and NATO: A Constructivist View on a National Interest and Alliance Behaviour," *Baltic Security and Defence Review*, Vol. 8, 2006, pp. 34-52.

2. In March 2010, the Baltic Defence College workshops featured presentations from the military staffs of all three Baltic nations as well as presentations of officers who had participated in deployments as commanders and staff officers.

3. For a Baltic view of the North Atlantic Treaty Organization (NATO) transformation and its significance, see Kestutis Paulauskas, "NATO at 60: Lost in Transformation," in *Lithuanian Annual Strategic Review 2009-2010*, Vilnius, Lithuania: Strategic Research Center, 2010, pp. 31-54; and Martynas Zapolskis, "NATO Transformation Scenarios" in *Lithuanian Annual Strategic Review 2009-2010*, Vilnius, Lithuania: Strategic Research Center, 2010, pp. 55-78.

4. For background on the security policy of the Baltic nations and their attitude towards NATO, see Zaneta Ozolina, ed., *Rethinking Security*, Riga, Latvia: Zinätne, 2010.

5. See Linas Linkevicius, Ambassador of Lithuania to NATO, "Participation of Lithuanian Troops in International Peace support Operations," *Baltic Defence Review*, Vol. 1, 1999, on Nordic nation support to the early Baltic forces. See also Major Aurelijus Alasauskas and Major Giedrius Anglickis, Lithuanian Army, "On the Baltic Experiences: Lithuanian Lessons Leaned from International Operations from 1994 to 2010," *Baltic Security and Defence Review*, Vol. 12, Issue 2, 2010, p.140, on the Swedish support to Baltic training.

6. Major Gunnar Havi, Estonian Army, "The Afghanistan Mission's Benefits for Estonia," *Baltic Security and Defence Review*, Vol. 12, Issue 2, 2010, p. 159.

7. General Michael Clemmeson, Danish Army, "NATO Interoperability and the Baltic Defence College," *Baltic Defence Review*, Vol. 1, 1999, pp. 1-7.

8. Linkevicius.

9. For a Baltic perception on the value of deployments as a means of developing the armed forces, see Havi. On early deployments, see pp. 159-161.

10. The importance of winning a seat at the table is a constant theme in the official statements and reports of the Baltic nations, as well as commentaries by leading political figures and academics. For Baltic attitudes and policy perceptions on NATO and the European Union (EU) commitment, see Margarita Seselgyte, "The Lithuanian Presidency of the EU Council and Common Security and Defense Policy: Opportunities and Challenges," in the *Lithuanian Annual Strategic Review 2011-2012*, Vol. 10, Vilnius, Lithuania: Strategic Research Center, 2012, pp. 87-120; Paulauskas, pp. 31-54; Egdunas Racius, "Lithuania in the NATO Mission in Afghanistan: Between Idealism and Pragmatism," *Lithuanian Annual Strategic Review 2009-2010*, Vilnius, Lithuania: Strategic Research Center, 2010, pp. 187-207; Martynas Zapolskis, "NATO Transformation Scenarios," *Lithuanian Annual Strategic Review 2009-2010*, Vilnius, Lithuania: Strategic Research Center, 2010, pp. 55-78; Zaneta Ozolina, "Measuring the Effectiveness of NATO," in *Rethinking Security*, Zaneta Ozolina, ed., Riga, Latvia: Zinätne, 2010, pp. 118-167.

11. Cited in Grazina Miniotaite, "The Construction of the Model of the Army in Lithuania's Political Discourse," in *Lithuanian Annual Strategic Review 2008*, Vilnius, Lithuania: Strategic Research Center, 2009, p. 196. The Lithuanian National Defence Strategy of 2004, upon joining NATO, strongly reaffirmed the membership of NATO and the centrality of collective security as the cornerstone of Lithuanian policy. *Lithuanian Annual Strategic Review 2011-2012*, Vol. 10, pp. 196-198.

12. Estonian Defence Ministry, *Estonian Long Term Defence Development Plan 2009-2018*, Tallinn, Estonia: Eesti Kaitsevägi, 2009, p. 3.

13. *Ibid.*

14. This was the case until the financial crisis of 2008. In 2009-11, all the Baltic budgets were cut. But in the 2012 and 2013 budgets, Estonia and Lithuania are increasing defense expenditures,

and Estonia is back on track to spend 2 percent of gross domestic product (GDP) on defense. The increasing defense budgets of the three Baltic States are in contrast with most Western European nations, which continue to decrease their military budgets.

15. For an excellent overview of all Lithuanian deployments, see Alasauskas and Anglickis, pp. 134- 158.

16. See Lithuanian Armed Forces, ed., *In Service for Peace*, Vilnius, Lithuania: Lithuanian Armed Forces, 2011, pp. 18-21, which details all the Lithuanian units and personnel that have deployed on overseas operations since 1994.

17. Proceedings of the Baltic Defence College Workshop on Baltic States' Deployment Experience, Tartu, Estonia, March 2010.

18. Alasauskas and Anglickis, p. 141.

19. The strong language capabilities of the Baltic armed forces come from the three Baltic nations' national education systems, which are high quality programs at all levels. Since 1991, English has been the second language of the Estonian, Lithuanian, and Latvian school systems. Most young people are somewhat fluent in English. As an adjunct professor of Tartu University, the author of this monograph teaches a graduate course to a highly multinational group completely in English. The author has regularly lectured in the University of Latvia in English and found that the undergraduates have exceptional fluency in English.

20. Captain Rene Toomse, Estonian Army, Report: *Lessons Learned, ESTHUMINT-2, Kandahar, Afghanistan, November 15, 2006-March 1, 2007*, Tallinn, Estonia, May 2010.

21. *Ibid.*

22. *Ibid.*

23. *Ibid.*

24. See Egdunas Racius, "The 'Cultural Awareness' Factor in the Activities of the Lithuanian PRT in Afghanistan," *Baltic Security and Defence Review*, Vol. 9, 2007, pp. 57-78.

25. Lieutenant Colonel Mindaugas Steponavicius, Lithuanian Army, "Lessons Learned for the Preparation of the ISAF Mission," June 2012.

26. *Ibid.*

27. On the laws authorizing the deployment of forces abroad, see Linkevicius.

28. *Strategy for the Engagement of the Republic of Lithuania in the International Community's Activities in the Islamic Republic of Afghanistan in 2009-2013,* Vilnius, Lithuania: Government of the Republic of Lithuania, 2009.

29. Major Giedrius Anglickis, Lithuanian Army, *Development of Local National Security forces and the Experience of Lithuania's Provincial Reconstruction Team, PRT, Mission in Afghanistan.* MA thesis of the Latvian National Defence Academy, Riga, Latvia, 2011 p. 8.

30. Baltic Defence College Workshop on Baltic Deployments, March 2010.

31. Anglickis, MA thesis, pp. 9-13.

32. Steponavicius, "Lessons Learned for the Preparation of the ISAF Mission."

33. Proceedings of the Baltic Defence College Workshop on Baltic States' Deployment Experience.

34. *Ibid.*

35. Lieutenant Colonel Mindaugas Steponavicius, "Lessons Learned in the Participation in the ISAF Operation," June 2012.

36. Proceedings of the Baltic Defence College Workshop on Baltic States' Deployment Experience.

37. Report of Lieutenant Colonel Darius Vaicikauskas, "Insights from the OSCE Mission in Kosovo," Kosovo Verification Mission, June 2012.

38. Proceedings of the Baltic Defence College Workshop on Baltic States' Deployment Experience.

39. *Ibid.*

40. *Ibid.*

41. See Havi, pp. 160-162; and Alasauskas and Anglickis, p. 137.

42. An excellent overview of how the Lithuanian PRT operated is General Almantas Leika, Lithuanian Army, who commanded the PRT 2006-2007, "The Lithuanian-led Provincial Reconstruction Team in Afghanistan — Achievements and Challenges," in *Lithuanian Annual Strategic Review 2008*, Vilnius, Lithuania: Strategic Research Center, 2009, pp. 161-182. The most extensive study of the doctrines the Lithuanians developed for Afghanistan counterinsurgency is Anglickis, MA thesis.

43. Proceedings of the Baltic Defence College Workshop on Baltic States' Deployment Experience.

ANNEX

Map of Afghanistan Provinces and Provincial Reconstruction Teams (PRTs). Lithuanian PRT Headquarters (HQ) was at Chaghcharan in West Central Afghanistan Marked by the Lithuanian Flag.

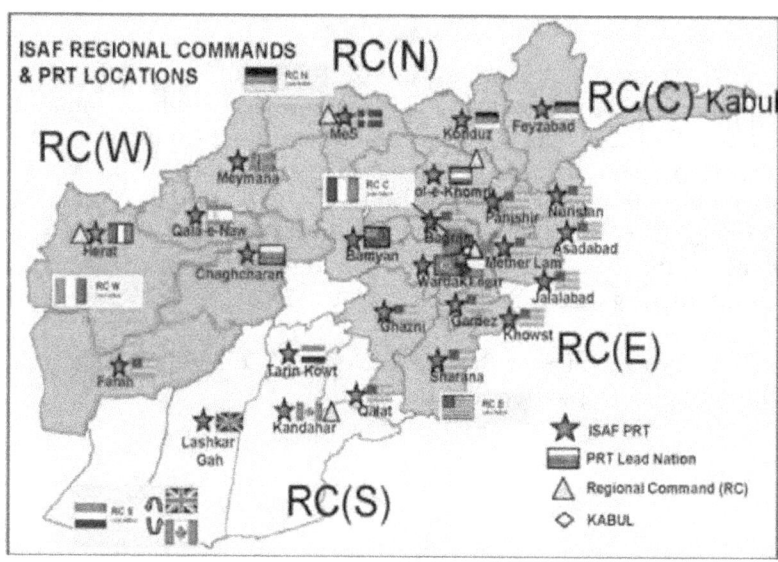

Figure 2. ISAF Provincial Reconstruction Team Locations.

www.ingramcontent.com/pod-product-compliance
Lightning Source LLC
Chambersburg PA
CBHW070232290526
45789CB00004B/1593